Polar Animals

Steve Bloom

This is me, Steve Bloom, with my camera ...

... and this seal is just one of the animals that we'll get to see!

The journey starts here ...

Thames & Hudson

Polar Animals

In search of polar bears, penguins, whales and seals

Steve Bloom

The expedition ...

6-7 Setting off ...

Meet your guide Steve Bloom. Find out where you are going and the amazing animals you'll see.

8-9 Polar north

Day 1 Head to the Arctic, one of the coldest places on Earth, and visit the frozen tundra.

▼ 10-11 A place of extremes

Days 2 to 5 Watch the sky to see a magical display of colour and get tips on surviving in your icy new home.

▼ 12-17 Nanook of the north

Days 6 to 15 On the trail of the king of the Arctic, the mighty polar bear.

12 Polar bear in close-up
14 Life on the ice
16 Growing up in the cold

Next, we spend time with playful polar bears.

The adventure starts with sky-watching in the polar north.

18-21 Whale watching

Days 16 to 17 Pack warm clothes for your whale-watching trip in the freezing Arctic waters.

18 Humpback whale in close-up
20 Feeding time

22-23 Changing seasons

Days 18 to 20 Keep your eyes open for an Arctic fox and meet some of the animals that visit for the brief but warm summer.

Then we travel south to the land of the penguins.

Our journey ends with seal spotting.

Setting off ...

Hi. I'm Steve Bloom, a wildlife photographer. I took the photos of the animals in this book. They all live in and around the harsh, icy lands near the North and South Poles. Join me on my adventure to capture these incredible survivors on camera in two of the most extreme places on Earth.

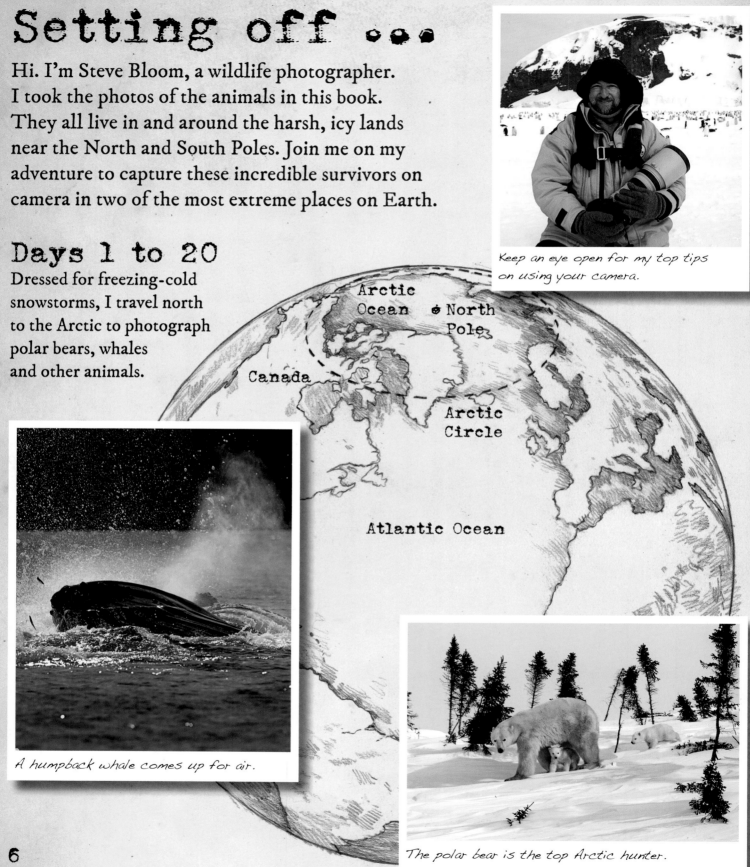

Keep an eye open for my top tips on using your camera.

Days 1 to 20

Dressed for freezing-cold snowstorms, I travel north to the Arctic to photograph polar bears, whales and other animals.

Arctic Ocean

North Pole

Canada

Arctic Circle

Atlantic Ocean

A humpback whale comes up for air.

The polar bear is the top Arctic hunter.

6

Days 21 to 40

Then I head south to Antarctica, a frozen continent where people have to live on special bases, protected from the severe weather. Here I meet penguins, seals and all kinds of birds.

This is an elephant seal, the largest of all seals.

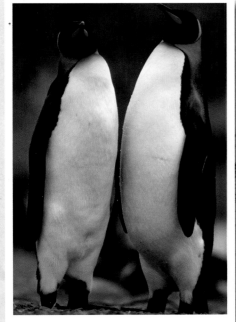

A pair of tall emperor penguins.

Skuas coming in to land on the frozen ocean.

Pacific Ocean

Antarctic Circle

Southern Ocean

Antarctica

South Pole

7

Polar north

Day 1

I arrive at the edge of the Arctic, a place so cold that the snow never melts all winter long. In the middle of this region there is a huge frozen ocean and around it a flat treeless land, known as tundra. I stand on the tundra and take my first picture – a reindeer. I wonder how animals can survive in this icy wilderness.

A place of extremes

Winter on the tundra is long and dark. During this time, the sun barely rises, creating an eerie twilight. In spring, the days begin to lengthen. Sometimes an incredible display fills the night sky with colors. This is called the Northern Lights.

For about a quarter of an hour, different-colored lights shift and swirl across the sky, making incredible patterns.

get used to my new
ne nights are clear,
s a chance I will
ights. When the
to flicker, I can
lieve it.

40 degrees below zero.

Fully dressed
In the freezing cold
you need to cover
every part of your
body. As well as a
thick, padded jacket,
I wear a mask to
protect my face
from frostbite.

Total whiteout
A blizzard can strike
in an instant, making it
impossible to see further
than the end of your nose.
This is called a whiteout.
I travel by snowmobile,
hoping that the weather
will improve enough
for me to take photos.

Skis work better than wheels on ice.

Luckily, there's no one to see me use it.

Toilet habits
Everyone needs to
go to the toilet,
even more so when
it's cold. I have
brought a toilet seat
and made a cozy fur
cover as a reminder
of home comforts.

11

Nanook of the north

Days 6 to 9

I head further north, deep into polar bear country. Polar bears may look cute, but they can be fierce. They are the world's largest meat-eating land animal. Mother bears are protective of their cubs and this one has cared well for her young. The word for polar bear in the language of the local Inuit people is *nanook*.

POLAR BEAR IN CLOSE-UP

Name:	*the scientific name for polar bear is* Ursus maritimus – *sea bear*
Found:	*in the Arctic region*
Weight:	*males – an average of 900 pounds*
	females – an average of 500 pounds
Height:	*up to 10 feet when standing upright on their back legs*
Favorite food:	*mainly seals, but also fish, reindeer and seabirds*
Lives for:	*25–30 years*
Number of young:	*usually two cubs at a time*

Underneath their light-colored fur, polar bears have black skin.

Life on the ice

Over the next few days, I follow a male polar bear as he roams the sea ice, hunting for food and looking for a mate. He will stay with her for only a few weeks before heading off again on his own.

When fighting, polar bears stand on their back legs, then bite and wrestle each other to the ground.

Day 10

A female bear is near by, and the male is following her tracks. When another male arrives, a fight breaks out. I capture the action on my camera. Polar bears fight viciously to win a mate. Sometimes the battles go on for over an hour, leaving the loser exhausted and hurt.

A polar bear has a powerful sense of smell.

Day 11

It's time for a snack, and seal meat is on the menu! A polar bear can sniff out a seal nearly one mile away, even if it's hiding under the ice. When food is less plentiful, the bear lives off its thick body fat.

On the hunt

Although polar bears are strong swimmers, they cannot match a seal's speed in the water. They have a better chance of catching one from the ice.

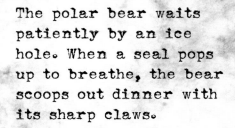

The polar bear waits patiently by an ice hole. When a seal pops up to breathe, the bear scoops out dinner with its sharp claws.

Day 12

The sea ice is beginning to break up and the seal-hunting season will soon be over. This is happening earlier and earlier each year in the Arctic. It's bad news for the polar bear, because the time it can spend hunting is getting shorter. Sadly, the polar bear's future is under threat.

As well as walking many miles, a polar bear will hitch rides on large floating pieces of ice, called ice floes.

Growing up in the cold

During the winter, polar bear cubs are born in snow caves dug out by the mother bear. She stays in the cave, feeding them a rich milk and watching them grow. When the weather warms in the spring, she takes them outside for the first time.

A mother and her two cubs warm themselves in the spring sunlight.

▲ Day 13

I am lucky to come across this family. The mother bear will look after her cubs for up to two-and-a-half years, teaching them all the skills they need to hunt and survive in this harsh wilderness.

Two young adults roll and tumble in the snow. They can playfight for hours!

Day 14 ▲

Today, I see two young adults playfighting. This is a great way to practice before they have to fight for real over a mate. I notice the rough and hairy soles of their oversized feet that help them to move easily across the slippery snow and ice. These animals are well adapted to their home.

Day 15 ▶

This polar bear has dug out a pit and buried itself in the snow to take a nap. It's the perfect way to keep warm and save energy. I leave it dozing inside its cozy blanket and say goodbye to these wonderful mammals.

A polar bear dozes for up to eight hours a day.

Splash! A humpback whale shows its powerful tail as it dives. The whale uses its tail to move through the water.

Whale watching

Day 16

My next stop is the Arctic Ocean. From nowhere a humpback whale rises, then dives back down into the icy water. I press the shutter and take a picture. These huge sea mammals are famous for singing beautiful songs that travel long distances through the water, helping them talk to one another and find mates.

HUMPBACK WHALE IN CLOSE-UP

Name:	the scientific name for humpback whale is Megaptera novaeangliae
Famous for:	watery gymnastics and noisy singing
Found:	near the surface in all the world's oceans
Body length:	about 50 feet (the length of a tractor-trailer)
Weight:	about 73,000 pounds (about the weight of a dump truck)
Favorite food:	krill (tiny sea creatures) and small fish
Lives for:	about 50 years
Number of young:	one calf every two or three years

Feeding time

Even though humpback whales have enormous mouths, they feast on only small fish and krill, which are tiny shrimp-like creatures. Their appetite for this food is huge!

Day 17

I can't believe my luck when I see a team of humpback whales working together to round up a school of fish. One whale blows bubbles around the fish to stop them from escaping, while the rest herd the fish into a circle. As they swim to the surface of the water, the whales gulp them all down. This technique is called bubble-net feeding.

Inside a mouth

If you look inside a humpback whale's mouth, you won't see any teeth. Instead, there are rows of comb-like plates made from a material called baleen.

The whale uses its mouth like a sieve. It scoops up a pile of fish along with lots of water. Then it filters out the water through the plates leaving the fish behind for it to swallow.

TOP TIPS

When taking pictures in the freezing cold, wear thin gloves covered with well-insulated fleece or leather gloves – and then mittens on top. Only take the mittens off briefly to work the camera!

21

Changing seasons

Days 18 to 20

My final days in the polar north are spent back on the tundra, where the snow is melting. I catch sight of an Arctic fox and focus my lens. Its thick fur coat changes color in spring, turning from white to brown to blend in with its surroundings.

An Arctic fox bounds across the land. It is one of the few animals that live here all year round.

SUMMER VISITORS

During the summer, when food is plentiful, many animals stop over in the Arctic.

Whooper swans gather in large flocks.

Whooper swan
These large birds are named after the loud whooping calls they make to one another. This photo shows them waiting out the winter in warm Japan. Next they will travel north to the Arctic to breed.

Horned puffin
Groups of puffins nest along the rocky coasts and dive offshore for tasty fish. A puffin travels the same route year after year to its nesting ground.

A puffin has webbed feet for swimming.

The whales fill their bellies with fish.

Humpback whale
Humpback whales swim up to 15,000 miles to reach their icy Arctic feeding grounds. They head to warmer waters for the winter and will not usually eat again until next year.

Polar

south

Day 21

My journey now takes me to Antarctica, the coldest, windiest and driest continent on Earth. Much of this hostile land is covered by a flat ice sheet many miles thick. Towering icebergs, some as large as whole countries, float in the surrounding ocean. As the sun rises, I spot a group of penguins perched on a drifting iceberg and focus my lens.

Penguin planet

Day 22

Along the icy coast, I am greeted by an impressive sight – a group of emperor penguins with their fluffy chicks. Different types of penguin live in and around Antarctica, but the emperor penguin is by far the largest. It is the only animal that can survive the whole winter on top of the ice in freezing, windswept conditions.

EMPEROR PENGUIN IN CLOSE-UP

Name :	*the scientific name for emperor penguin is* Aptenodytes forsteri
Found :	*in the Antarctic region*
Weight :	*up to 90 pounds*
Height :	*up to 45 inches*
Favorite food :	*fish, squid, krill and crustaceans*
Lives for :	*up to 20 years*
Number of young :	*lays one egg at a time*

Fluffy downy feathers keep these emperor penguin chicks warm.

Happy families

Days 23 to 27

Over the next few days, I spend time with a colony of Adélie penguins. It's a noisy, smelly place, with thousands of families closely packed together. Here the birds lay their eggs and raise their chicks. An Adélie penguin treks many miles to its nesting ground, searching out the same mate year after year.

Two Adélie penguins stop for a kiss! They can recognize each other by touch and through calls, even after they have spent many months apart.

FROM EGG TO CHICK

Penguins have developed clever ways to look after their eggs and give their chicks the best chance of survival. Take a look at my photo story.

The egg is protected by a flap of skin.

Keep it warm

A female king penguin lays one egg. Both parents take turns to keep it warm by resting it on their feet. When the egg hatches, one parent looks after the chick while the other heads off to find it tasty fish.

Let's stick together

As the chick grows, the parents spend more time away. All the young birds huddle together in a busy nursery for protection.

It can be difficult spotting your own chick in the crowd!

The transformation is nearly complete.

A new coat

After about nine months, the chick loses its downy feathers and gets a proper waterproof coat. Now is the time for the young penguin to take its first dive into the water and swim off to catch its own food.

29

On the move

Day 28

Although a penguin is a bird, it cannot fly. Instead, it zooms through the water at high speed and waddles around slowly and clumsily on land. A penguin has a few other clever tricks for getting around. Today I saw them in action.

An emperor penguin takes a flying leap.

Up and away

In the water, a penguin almost 'flies' along using its flippers. It travels with such speed and power that it can shoot itself up onto the ice without pausing for a second. This is a handy way of escaping enemies such as seals.

Penguin parade

As well as the king, emperor and Adélie penguins you have met so far, there are other types of penguins to get to know. Take a look at my photo album. These penguins all nest further north on the islands around Antarctica. Can you spot the differences between them?

A chinstrap penguin looks like it's wearing a tight-fitting helmet with a strap.

Why walk when you can slide in style? This emperor penguin goes for a ride.

▲ Slip and slide

Later that day, I spot this penguin gliding along the ice on its belly. It uses its feet and flippers to push itself forwards. Traveling like this is called tobogganing. It's a quick way to move about!

A rockhopper penguin has yellow feathers on its head that look like bushy eyebrows.

A macaroni penguin has feathers on its head, too. It's larger than a rockhopper penguin.

Flying high

Day 29

Today, I look up and focus my camera on the sky. Above me, a wandering albatross soars through the air. This majestic creature has the largest wingspan of any bird. It's much wider than your outstretched arms. It spends most of its life at sea, only coming to land to raise its chicks.

WANDERING ALBATROSS IN CLOSE-UP

Name: the scientific name for wandering albatross is Diomedea exulans

Found: in the Antarctic region

Weight: up to 22 pounds

Wingspan: up to 11 feet

Favorite food: squid, octopus, cuttlefish and crustaceans

Lives for: up to 80 years

Number of young: lays one egg at a time

A wandering albatross can fly over 600 miles in one day.

Raising chicks

Over the next two days, I watch a colony of black-browed albatrosses looking after their chicks. The birds nest on steep cliffs so they can glide off into the air and out to sea to find food.

Day 30

A female black-browed albatross lays one large egg. The male builds a sturdy nest from mud, seaweed and bird poo for her to sit in and keep the egg warm. When the chick hatches, looking after it is a full-time job so both parents work together.

This albatross chick will stay in its nest for up to five months.

Mates for life

Albatrosses usually pair up for life. On another of my travels, I was lucky enough to catch sight of a male wandering albatross trying to find a mate. The bird stretched out its impressive wings while two females watched. Then it started to dance, lifting and bowing its head. It made lots of noises too. I found myself completely fascinated by this show-off, but I still managed to take a picture!

Which female do you think will be most impressed?

34

This albatross has just finished feeding her young chick a rich oil, which she poured from her bill into its open mouth. The oil is made from fish and squid she has eaten earlier. It gives the chick energy in the cold and helps it to grow quickly.

A caring mother albatross checks on her chick and gives it a nudge with her bill.

Bird gallery

Days 32 to 35

I spend time with the other seabirds along the coast. Thousands of birds flock south in spring when food is more plentiful and the weather is less chilly. Here are just a few of the different types I photographed.

Skua ▷

A penguin needs to watch out when there is a skua about. Given the chance, this cheeky bird will think nothing of stealing a penguin egg or even a baby chick to eat! It also flies after other seabirds, trying to force them to drop their catch in mid-air.

A skua, perched on a rock, keeps its eye open for a tasty snack.

In the breeding season, the yellow bump on the king cormorant's beak gets even brighter.

◁ King cormorant

You can easily recognize a king cormorant by its glossy black feathers and the bright yellow bump at the top of its beak. This large seabird is an excellent diver. Underwater it uses its powerful webbed feet to swim down and search out fish.

A snow petrel comes in to land on the icy water.

◀ Snow petrel

This snow petrel is about the same size as a pigeon. It dives for fish in the waters around Antarctica but it has also been spotted flying as far south as the icy pole. A snow petrel has a gruesome way of defending itself. When threatened, it throws up a stinky fish oil over its attacker.

Kelp gull ▶

Kelp gulls fly all over the southern half of the world. They feast on anything they can find, even pecking at live whales to get at their flesh.

Top Tips

When taking pictures of birds at rest, keep quiet and try not to disturb them. Otherwise, they may fly off before you get the shot.

When I took this picture of a kelp gull in flight, I kept its eye in the frame and followed it with the camera.

Sleek and shiny

Day 36

My final days in Antarctica are spent seal watching. Several types of seal swim in the icy waters here. This one I photographed is an Antarctic fur seal. It has a sleek, streamlined body and two small ear flaps on the side of its head. Although seals sometimes rest on the ice, they often stay at sea for weeks at a time swimming and diving for food.

ANTARCTIC FUR SEAL IN CLOSE-UP

Name : *the scientific name for Antarctic fur seal is* Arctocephalus gazella

Found : *in the Antarctic region*

Weight : *males – up to 500 pounds*
females – up to 110 pounds

Length : *males – up to 6.5 feet*
females – up to 5 feet

Favorite food : *fish, squid, birds and krill*

Lives for : *up to 30 years*

Number of young : *one pup at a time*

An Antarctic fur seal has sharp eyesight and hearing to

help it find its dinner. Some scientists think that it uses its whiskers to sense prey too.

Two male elephant seals roar loudly at one another. They will bite and wrestle as well until one leaves defeated.

Go away!

Day 37

Every year, enormous elephant seals head to the shore to breed. The males fight over an area of beach and a large group of females. As the action heats up, I take care not to come too close. Finally I get the picture I have been waiting for.

Life on the coast

Days 38 to 40

Before I say goodbye to the seals and leave Antarctica,
I watch their daily lives, marveling at how well they
are adapted to survive in their icy, watery world.

Two Antarctic fur seals come up for air during a fight!

◀ Up for air

A seal can hold its breath for
up to two hours under water
as it swims and dives down
to hunt for fish. But seals
are mammals, so they must
come to the surface of the
water to breathe air.

Fierce ▶ predator

The leopard seal is
the top hunter in
Antarctica after the
killer whale. It feeds
on fish, penguins and
even other seals.

This leopard seal might look cute, but its mouth hides rows of sharp teeth.

How a seal swims

An Antarctic fur seal swims using its front flippers to push itself along. True seals, which include leopard seals and elephant seals, use their back flippers. They have more streamlined bodies and swim longer distances. This picture shows a leopard seal swimming.

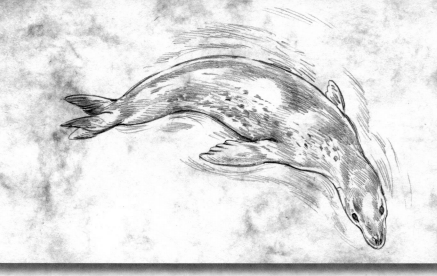

▼ Growing pup

On the shore, a fur seal pup waits for its mother. It's a dangerous time alone. When the mother returns, she will feed it her rich, fatty milk to help it grow quickly. At the age of about four months, the pup will be big enough to fend for itself.

A seal pup can recognize its mother by smell.

Steve's photo tips

I was lucky enough to visit the icy polar lands to take my photos, but you can get brilliant shots of animals and nature closer to home. Check out my tips, then head to the park or take a family trip to a nature reserve with your camera.

1. Shoot ▶ a landscape

When photographing a landscape, it's a good idea to have a large interesting object in the picture to draw in your eye. You can also include animals or people to give a sense of scale and make things look more impressive.

The Adélie penguins give you an idea of just how big this floating block of ice really is!

Here, I tried to convey the power and magnificence of a polar bear.

◀ 2. Take a portrait

With a portrait, try to capture an animal's unique look and personality. Keep the background simple so it does not become too distracting and the animal remains the focus. Instead of a polar bear, you could photograph a family pet.

This photo is divided into three clear areas – the rock, the puffins and the grass.

3. Work with a group ▲

When taking pictures of a group of animals, think about how all the parts of the photo will work together. I kept the puffins in the foreground, then framed them with the lush green grass.

4. Capture ▶ action

Photographing animals in action can be tricky and is often a combination of patience and luck. Watch the animal closely and be ready to press the camera shutter at the right time. Don't worry if you get it wrong, you can always try again and delete the photos you don't want.

The splashing water around this chinstrap penguin adds to the sense of movement.

Photo projects

Here are some of my favorite projects to help you have fun with your pictures and develop your camera skills. To become a good photographer takes lots of practice, but it is well worth putting in the effort.

Birthday card ▷

Add a personal touch to a birthday card by making it yourself and including one of your photos. Simply take a piece of heavy paper, fold it in half and stick on the picture. Write a caption or design one on the computer. Your friend will be really impressed!

Happy Birthday!

MY BIRD SPOTTING GUIDE

Name: dolphin gull

Spotted: November

Markings: gray throat, red beak

Where: rocky beach

MORE TOP TIPS

* I took my photos with fancy equipment, but a simple digital camera is a great way to start.

◁ Wildlife ID guide

Are you wild about birds, insects, dogs or other animals? Then, how about designing an ID guide for them? Try to show the creature's markings clearly in the photo and note where you saw the animal. If you're not sure of the species, look in a reference book to find out.

1. Collecting dried grass

2. Nest-building under way

3. Nearly there!

Action sequence △

Shooting an action sequence with an animal can be a challenge, but don't give up. Take lots of pictures, then decide later on the best ones to use and the order to put them in. You can always stage an action sequence with people or toys.

Picture postcards ▽▷

To make a postcard, add a speech bubble and caption on the computer, then print it out on a card. Think about the mood of the photo — is it funny or dramatic? Is there a story behind the picture that you can tell?

Time for a bath!

A family of chinstrap penguins covered in mud and penguin poo

Yawn.

Two elephant seals relax on the ice

47

Index

For my son Adam

Photographs copyright © 2012 Steve Bloom
stevebloom.com
Text copyright © 2012 Thames & Hudson Ltd, London
Illustrations copyright © 2012 Thames & Hudson Ltd, London
Illustrations by Peter Bull
Researched and edited by Deborah Kespert
Consultant Barbara Taylor

The right of Steve Bloom to be identified as the
photographer of this work has been asserted under
the Copyright, Designs and Patents Act 1988

First published in 2012 in hardcover in the
United States of America by Thames & Hudson Inc.,
500 Fifth Avenue, New York, New York 10110

thamesandhudsonusa.com

Library of Congress Catalog Card Number 2012931640

ISBN 978-0-500-65011-0

Published in Great Britain under the title
My Polar Animals Journal

Printed and bound in China by C&C Offset Printing Co. Ltd

penguin

polar bear

seal